NEW AGE COIN

New Age Coin

Money is Constantly Evolving, Shouldn't You?

MVCVM

Dedication

I'd like to thank my girlfriend, Hannah,
for supporting every effort I make to
give something back to not only her but
everyone else that wishes to find
knowledge & a new adventure.

Contents

Intro

Throughout this text we will cover from top-to-bottom what cryptocurrency actually is & how to tangibly use it. Under no notion am I giving you financial or investment advice, I am simply breaking down the entire understanding of cryptocurrency ("crypto" for short) and everything you need to be digitally literate in the new space that we are moving towards as a whole. The world is constantly evolving and we have to keep up. On that notion, I figured I'd find a way to help you out by giving you the most solid foundation that I can before you venture out on your own into the wilds of the Digital Age.

Bitcoin is regarded as the first cryptocurrency & created by Satoshi Nakamoto. The likes of Satoshi are not known, whether he actually exists as a person or the name was created as an acronym for a group that developed the product. Ever since the adoption of Bitcoin many other cryptos have begun springing up withing the digital realm to either act as scamming money grabs or viable solutions to the evolving challenges that a new system creates as it grows larger & more mainstream.

One thing I must point out is that every single crypto that you use can & will be tracked. Bitcoin, Etherium, Ripple, Binance Token, all of them leave a trail of who used and held them in what wallet. If you are privacy minded &

focused, later in the book I'll give a look at how to masks what you use and where you use it.

* * *

DISCLAIMER: By no means am I a financial advisor or assets manager. I take no responsibility for what you do with your finances. I am not a licensed digital security consultant either. I have merely spent the time finding resources & groups to expand my knowledge & I wish to share the findings with you and make your life easier in the process.

Section 1:
Cryptocurrencies &
What Makes Them

Chapter 1

What is Crypto?

Cryptocurrency or "Crypto," is one of the most exciting, alluring, & seemingly mysterious markets man has seemed to create so far. Relatively new & in the early-adoption phase (about 10 years old now in 2021), it has become more and more prominent in daily life. We have gone from having almost no way of buying into anything to now being able to sync our bank accounts to online exchanges and even through simply 1-click purchases like Cash App. At this point we all have to know that crypto is here to stay and will continue to expand as long as we have a growing technological civilization and the world becomes more and more connected. This situation ends up being known as DeFi or Decentralized Finance, since most mainstream banks are not involved & the funds are in control of you, the user.

The fundamental foundation of a cryptocurrency is simply called the "Blockchain." Think of a blockchain as, what its name is, a series of blocks strewn together. In computer speak a block is a chunk of encrypted data, that gets read, processed, packaged up using cryptography, & keeps records of the transaction info in a specific timestamp that then gets attached to the previous block creating a chain. Each chain is then kept on a connected ledger that keeps track of every transaction ever made with each coin & fraction of a coin between coin exchanges & wallets. We will come back to these details later in this section.

Computers have to download a specific software in order to "mine" the crypto from the ledgers. The way mining works is every computer in a network piles into groups called "pools." Now pools require all of this computing power put together to mine each byte of data being held on these ledgers in order to properly record and create a 1:1 ratio for sending & receiving a transaction. This process is ultimately what the banks & 3rd party payment processors have been doing with credit/debit cards. The banks can't verify quickly enough that you had spent $3 at the gas station so they rely on an intermediary to verify the purchase and take the initial hit of the funds spent. Often times this can lead to "double spending" as it is referred to. Double spending is when your account shows that a transaction was charged for the same amount or charged for more than it has in the account itself. What the blockchain system has done is ultimately eliminate the double spending effect of delayed payment systems.

Cryptocurrencies are broken down into fractional amounts regarding whatever fiat currency you are used to using (fiat being a government issued currency not backed by any physical means; gold, silver, etc.). For example in the U.S. everything is compared to $ 0.00 amounts; whole numbers can infinitely go up while fractional amounts go to .00000001, 8 decimals right of the 0. These are the smallest fraction of value that a crypto is broken down to & is often called by the name of the creator. Bitcoin's alleged creator was Satoshi Nakamoto therefore the smallest unit is called a Satoshi & such follows for other coins like Etherium, etc.

Contracts happen to be the root code to building new cryptos & any apps that pair along with them. Etherium uses a baseline of ERC20 which allows all new coins to be built along the Etherium blockchain which makes these transactions far faster than those with standard Bitcoin. Lesser known coins have locations for the initial code to be found so that way your wallet can adopt the coin an act as a node (place of storage) on the blockchain network for the coin. Contracts let developers constantly add to the tangibility or new coins on networks and consistently expand the marketplace.

Chapter 2

Fees

With the guaranteed aspect of verifying a transaction however, there are trade-offs. Yes, everyone receives their funds in whatever form of coin or token they may be transacting with but now there are constant fees & subsequent time delays that are greatly inconvenient. The fees range in price depending on the coin, type of transaction, speed of the transaction, & priority of the transaction. The most common terms for fees are: transaction fee, gas fee, exchange fee, & many more depending on the platform. Transaction fees are simply that, they pay for the sending of funds from buyer to seller for the price of exchange between the 2 parties.

Gas fees are the % of funds from the transaction to pay the blockchain miners for hosting their resources to complete the blockchain transactions. The gas fees have a typical baseline amount in which the type of coin has predetermined depending on numerous factors such as the popularity, complexity of code within the blockchain, accuracy of slippage between coin pair prices, amount of coin exchanged, & so forth. Gas fees can be higher for coins such as Bitcoin since after each transaction the chain ultimately destroys a fraction of the coin from the total amount in the world & makes the blockchain far more complex. These fees can also be throttled up & down depending on how long you want to wait, obviously faster costs more because of bumping your priority up in the ledger & using more miners at once.

Exchange fees work almost in the same way as transaction fees however, they are most often used on an exchange platform in order to exchange one coin for the opposite one in a pairing. An example would be Bitcoin/USDT: where you want to trade your USD Token to the equal amount in Bitcoin. Due to these being held within the Centralized (CEX)(federally regulated) & De-Centralized (DEX)(non regulated) exchanges there are often times no other fees since you are simply moving around internal wallet structures within the host platform. There are limits to how small of a coins value can be moved and exchanged within every platform. Often times you end up left with a hyper fraction of a coin being left in the previous wallet after most transactions. Due to this amount being minimal, you as the user will more than likely never actually lose more than a couple fractions of a cent over a series of time.

Chapter 3

Wallets

All crypto will be stored in a form of a wallet somewhere on some device. As this is a digital object therefore every device has to be digital, store on a form of computer hard drive, & be able to communicate to the blockchain after syncing. Wallets come in all forms; both hardware & software with software being the most popular and easy to use. Software wallets come as applications as anything else does on a device & each device holds the key to your crypto wallet which syncs to the blockchain to verify funds. A branched form of software storage for the user are the new companies that have formed "crypto-banks" as I call them.

Basic software wallets include some of the most popular such a Cake Wallet, which lets you store the most popular cryptos & exchange within the app itself to mask the exchange addresses slightly, with its amount of fees of course. Then others such as MetaMask which can be turned on & off as a browser extension that syncs to an app on your phone. What I like about MetaMask is that it can easily help you obtain the contract info of the type of coin, if not supported, and add it to the wallet to store. There are various other wallets with more popularity out there such as Exodus and at that point its all about what you the user like to hold on your device. Remember, security is always a concern with every wallet & device that has access to your keys. Everything can be hacked or include malware so be sure to do your due diligence before hopping on the next trend of wallets.

Banking wallets act as physical banks do in the real world; they store your value of currency, pay you a % of interest & lend your money out to other borrowers to generate revenue. An advantage that the crypto banks have is that unlike a traditional banking system where you're basically punished for storing your fiat, crypto banks pay extremely high daily compounding %APY. The ones I personally use the most are Nexo, BlockFi, & Crypto.com. These companies let you store value, borrow against your assets without actually spending the asset amount & pay back what you borrowed on your terms with minimal interest compared to physical banks. I go over how to use these as financial hacks depending on how you report your taxes and include your crypto at the end of the year against money borrowed in the process in my online courses.

Physical wallets, often called cold wallets, are basically USB drives on steroids which are specifically designed to store your crypto & its keys. It's amazing to think that one of these can store millions of dollars of cryptocurrency within them and be no larger than a jump drive. These are often for the rich and or paranoid as they offer the utmost security in case of a data breach or hacking within one of the other platforms provided. You have literally 0 risk of your money being stolen without your knowledge as these can be attached to your physical being at all times or locked away in a vault. Along with the ultimate privacy of carrying around your funds, however you divvy them up, these wallets can adopt any contract of a crypto if it isn't initially support & usually let you send your coins to an exchange from your laptop. The most popular form of these is the Ledger brand, no I do not have a sponsorship by them, they are simply the most popular. Ledger comes included with its own exchange so you can lot however many coins into each crypto category you wish.

Chapter 4

Value

Crypto was once seen as a gimmick and merely a way to exchange money in an alternate form. Having learned about it tangibility & acceptance into the market people now offer viable ways of exchanging their funds for services & objects. Being adopted by the masses as the first way to make money on exchanges and avoid tax in ways crypto had seen its initial boom within the last 5 years. The saying always goes; "as long as there is demand the value will go up."

Moving on to a form of accepted store of value, the big governments of the world began to take their steps to finding people who were purchasing and exchanging these tokens without properly reporting them to the entities such as the IRS. Now that digital value was obtainable through decoding of the public ledgers, people could now be tracked from their purchases & to every wallet that their coin had been moved to.

Calculating actual value of crypto is key to understanding the markets and trends. Market Cap is the general term for the value of the whole market at the time & the #1 resource for this is the website coinmarketcap.com. Here all cryptos are listed in ranks defining the factors of their entire market. Circulating supply is used as an estimate regarding the number of coins within the market & public wallets. Total supply is used as an estimate of total coins reduced by coins that have been burned (burned means the currency was destroyed or removed from the system which creates more scarcity). Max supply simply means the number of coins that have ever existed within the lifetime of the currency. The formula for calculating market cap is as follows:

Price * Circulating Supply
or
Total Current Coins * Current Price

These prices can be manipulated through a process of "wash trading," as it's called. Wash trading is when parties sell currency between themselves to give the perceived view of active movement going on in the market. This process artificially inflates the price because one party sells the currency then the other party sells the currency back at an inflated price, then they repeat until a solid percentage increase has occurred, driving the overall market price up.

Volume of a coin is simply the number of active trades that occur regarding said coin. Same as with stocks or forex markets, the larger the volume the better it is for the market due to more resources being readily available for trading. If

Bitcoin has $100 million in trading volume & the price is $10,000 per Bitcoin, then there are roughly 10,000 Bitcoin being traded within the market. Volume is a strong metric of measuring how healthy a coin's following and investment/trading probably of profit could possible be.

Be weary of the halving process that occurs in some of the currencies. What was most known regarding Bitcoin & its halving were the mining rewards. With the coin structure being split into half essentially, this created a higher difficulty of mining and reducing the rewards for mining the currency's blockchain. With increased difficulty of mining rewards and typical price increase after each of these you will begin to see a scarcity effect blanket the market. Naturally, less coin is exchanged so price goes up.

I go over this information in far more detail on my web courses over at **newagecoin.net**.

Section 2:
Purchasing, Exchanging, Leveraging & Tax Structure

Chapter 5

Types of Exchanges

For most Americans, the largest exchange platforms that they can easily purchase crypto at are Coinbase (I do not recommend Coinbase because they stole from their users), Binance, Kraken, & Crypto.com. All of these are considered CEX or Centralized Exchanges with the opposite of that being a DEX, or DE-Centralized Exchange. Naturally, centralized have government regulation procedures, insurance, proof of funds, ID verification (KYC) and everything offered with a regulated entity. These are places that offer security in the exchange of privacy, so if you're cool with your ID and info being shoved into another government database go right ahead. DE-centralized exchanges however, are what you could easily guess, not controlled by a government. These places often require a reputation behind them after people have been using them for some time and they gain trust for being straightforward as anything else. Most people use Uniswap as their main platform to quickly exchange between currencies and platforms to find certain pairings of coins or one you usually can't find on a central exchange.

Make sure to go into most exchanges without making an account, or by using a single-use email such as a ProtonMail account. Then by generating a VPN in a privacy based browser such a Firefox or Brave. We cover more details regarding specific setting in these throughout my online course on exchanges and privacy focus. In most cases of VPN use always choose a country that will have English as a language option naturally. Countries such as England, France, Japan, Australia, etc., so this way you don't have to deal with the strict KYC or even making an account on these central platforms and risk your identity getting tracked.

General American exchanges are usually considered safe purchasing platforms, meaning you can sync a bank account or card to the system to charge you for however much you with to deposit and purchase in crypto. Be made aware though, these platforms report every single transaction to the IRS. Purchases, send, receive, exchange, & sale of crypto is bound to all IRS tax laws. We'll cover the US tax structure later in this section. Coinbase, Binance, Crypto.com, Gemini, Uphold, all count as standard exchanges that track every move you make with cryptocurrencies and will report to the IRS because they want the money of being compliant. Atypical platforms consist of those such as Cash App, where you may only purchase Bitcoin and use it as payment or send and receive. This also reports to the IRS on crypto transactions. Each one of these involves a KYC process or "Know Your Customer." Due to the violating Patriot Act signed into place back in the early 2000's every financial institution is now required to KYC every single user. This process requires all personal info along with ID & face verification which is then saved into national databases that are shared throughout the U.S. government and used against every American for tax purposes.

Take note: *Any funds left in an exchange are not technically yours. Since these funds are held in the exchange's wallet even though it has your name on it, they are still not actually your wallet. Remember the saying, "Not your keys, not your wallet." As you have to own the recovery key & login info to actually own the wallet outright.*

Chapter 6

Making Crypto Work for You

All the time in the investment world you hear about making your money work for you to make more money. Well in these still early stages of crypto there are far greater returns to be made due to the liquidity of the markets. Depending on your tech skills, computing power, internet speed, & knowledge of the markets there are several machines in which to make solid growth with crypto.

The most explosive (high-risk, high-reward) is the typical leverage trading. You see all the time in the stock markets with leveraged shares or leveraged options where the big hedge funds either exponentially add money or lose it, well same thing goes for crypto. Because you are now borrowing funds on a % value you have the chance to read the charts and cash out or lose big. Naturally since you're using other people's money you have to get through a centralized exchange in your country and fully KYC, being subject to the tax structure of where you live regarding crypto.

Secondly we have less aggressive approaches regarding mining or joining liquidity pools & staking. Mining and pools sort of go together as they're almost the same thing. Mining is when you have a computer pitching to calculate all of the hashes of the transactions, as I explained earlier in the text. This is generally pretty stable depending on the currency the crypto is in, except with Bitcoin, as it gets slower over time due to the complexity of the mining. Next is joining a mining pool where that is simply sending your computing power to join a group of other computers to all speed up the hashing on the blockchain to get paid quicker but with a faster rate of mining reward. 3rd off, there are the companies such as exchanges, crypto banks, & loaning services where you can stake funds. Each of them gives you a daily compounding %APY based on the value of what crypto that you had staked for them to sell loans. This is simply using your money to loan to a 3rd party and they pay you interest off of it. Other companies let you do a mix of pools and staking such as Cake but that gets complicated because you need to stake a certain ratio of the funds into each pool in order to get paid & it really is bad for the market health to make such controlled funding off of that process.

Lastly, the easiest way to make passive %APY is by leaving your funds in a "crypto bank." Nexo is my personal favorite as they are off-shore of the US, then there are others such as Crypto.com & BlockFi. We'll use Nexo since I have before as the example. Nexo lets you send any of the mainstream cryptos to their platform in your account; Bitcoin, ETH, XRP, XLM, USDT, British Pound, Euro, etc. Simply by sitting there you get paid a daily compounding %APY of a minimum 4% which is paid back as the crypto in the account. Stablecoins such as the fiat currency coins get 8% APY since they aren't near as volatile due to them being synced up to a countries currency. What's really nice about platforms like Nexo & BlockFi is that they have programs where you get paid to leave your money in their accounts while at the same time you can borrow against your assets. So what Nexo does is it has a set % rate for each coin you may borrow against. Stablecoins have a 90% LTV (loan to value), BTC has about a 60%, & more volatile coins such as XRP have a 40%. So if you have $1000 in USDT in your account you may now borrow $900 against it as a bank wire into your regular bank account. These loans are on your terms, generally called at 1-year however, you may contact Nexo and negotiate with them a time extension. Since you now have a $900 loan from Nexo you only pay interest on the days you borrow & that interest is subtracted from the interest you gain from your assets. Basically as long as your assets in holding generate more gained interest than your borrowed interest you won't have to pay more than what you borrowed plus the first month's interest. This is a great tool, since most of us will borrow money anyway, why not make it on your terms and have your money grow with you? It's basically an infinite money financial hack.

If you really would like to know more infinite money hacks simply contact me through the website & I'll show you how to use crypto and other tools such as your own insurance policies to not only make money, but keep all of the money you earn in a money making machinne.

Chapter 7

Crypto Tax Structure

Once again the land of the free is taxed to death on another asset. Understanding crypto taxes and what can happen depending on what is bought, sold, exchanged or HODL'd when & where is key. Once again, understand that every cryptocurrency except a select few are completely public & you have to understand what you were doing with your currencies & what wallets you're storing them in. That being said, let's go over the current US tax structure regarding crypto.

As of May 2021 the US treats crypto as property; the same category as stocks, bonds, & real estate. This is generally subject to capital gains tax however there is one catch with the crypto. If crypto is earned as income from a job or mining then it is treated as income and subject to income tax withholding. So once again the government has created a deterrent to someone wanting to use a coin they don't have solid regulation over.

So crypto is taxed when:

- Trading crypto to fiat
- Trading/exchanging from one crypto to another
- Spending crypto on goods or services
- Earning crypto as income

Not taxed:

- Buy & hold (HODL)
- Wallet to wallet (send from one wallet to another you own)

Cryptotrader.tax gives you a full-dive analysis of how the taxes and examples would be broken down if you wish to hang around there for a few minutes & study the structure. They also offer a tax plug-in which you could use for your Binance or Coinbase purchases anyway. It will digitally track every purchase & sending transaction within the exchange application & report your taxes for you if you're really up-tight about being a straight laced citizen for the fed.

There are also crypto tax haven countries out there that want people to have some financial freedom or be completely separate from their tax and banking system.

List of countries:

- Belarus: no capital gains on crypto until 2023
- Bermuda: no tax on income or capital gains including cryptocurrencies
- British Virgin Islands: no capital, income, or corp tax for those who reside therefore
- Cayman Islands: no crypto tax
- Germany: 0% crypto gains tax if held for 1+ years
- Malta: no capital gains for foreign business, 5% on residential corps, however still part of EU
- Panama: No capital gains on crypto for non-Panama sourced gains
- Peru: 5% capital gains tax
- Portugal: no individual capital gains unless trading full time as a business
- Puerto Rico: 0 capital gains on crypto, ACT 22 tax incentive
- Singapore: 0% crypto capital gains, short-term profit taxed as ordinary income

There are certain ways around certain tax processes which I don't recommend you do unless you go through every legal loophole or you're best friends with a politician to get you out of a jam. For educational purposes we will go over what to avoid.

- Avoid using the VPN & non-KYC, decentralized exchange as a deposit wallet & exchange for an untraceable coin such as Monero. Then either exchange the

Monero back into another coin and send it off-shore or keep the Monero.

· If you were to have the resources between a large enough group, that group could possibly set up shop as a mining operation within a foreign entity and be owned either internally as someone moved to a tax haven and operated under the tax laws stated earlier from the havens listed.

· Some of these people could even use the U.S. financial legal structure against itself by setting up a foreign business in such a place like a dual-purpose fiat & crypto tax haven. Set up a proper corporation within that haven, build portfolios & bank accounts for each individual party that you wish to do business with then help them transfer funds over. Technically the foreign business would act as a service or simply selling products at a negotiated price as such, the U.S. business would pay for the service or product at it's premium, wire the funds to the foreign business, write the fees off on their IRS tax form, then having created a customer service account through the foreign entity have access to their funds which are automatically (as part of the agreement) invested into crypto with the company's money. The foreign company pays is typical income tax structure to keep the local government happy but this is fine since it's not the overreaching U.S. tax entity. The funds are then moved into a portfolio within the company and the alleged person who would own the funds now has access to the crypto. Naturally the host company would take a fee and use this for day trading & internal jobs & what not.

But hey, I want everyone to be creative in the ways they figure things out on what to avoid doing. Always know & understand your local tax laws and how they can transcend borders, understand crypto, payment processing, mining, the whole picture. We are obviously moving towards digital currency & assets & I want each and every one of you to understand the game. Knowledge is power, use the rules against themselves, & stay ahead. This is the next big market so I want you to be on the forefront of what's going down.

Section 3: Obtaining Monero (XMR)

* * *

Know this, Monero is the key to a people's free & sovereign crypto future. It is not evil, it is fungible & the government hates it because they cannot track or tax it. Begin researching exchanges and platforms using the methods I've given to get your hands on as much Monero as you can. Monero is the way of the people.

* * *

Step-by-step of ways to obtain Monero:

1. Create Coinbase/Binance/Kraken/Gemini
    - Register through entire KYC process
    - Verify identity for the government & tax purposes
    - Sync bank account and/or credit/debit card
2. Purchase coins such as Ethereum, Litecoin, USD coins, Stellar for lower fees & high speed

3. Go to getmonero.org & download the desktop GUI wallet
   - Preciously save the key-phrase with your life, this the only way to backup your wallet
4. Download Cake Wallet (cakewallet.com)
   - In Cake Wallet go to: Menu > Wallets > Create New Wallet > create Monero Wallet
   - Repeat for Litecoin Wallet as well
   - Swipe left to view your wallet deposit address & deposit QR code
   - Save key-phrases with your life
   - Send Bitcoin or Litecoin to Cake Wallet to convert in-app to XMR
5. DO NOT 2-STEP AUTHORIZE ANY ACCOUNTS FROM THIS POINT ON
6. Active VPN service to show computer and browser in another country
   - Choose a private browser with new private window for more security to avoid cookies & fingerprinting
7. With VPN active, create single-use email through Proton / StartMail / CTemplar
8. Create an email only account through VPN in exchanges such as Binance /Poloniex / CEX
9. Send other coins to exchanges if you need to exchangefrom coins not supported in Cake Wallet
   - Find matching pairs by searching the Exchanges tab within the platforms
   - Look for XMR pairs
   - Export to GUI or Cake Wallet
   - DO NOT leave funds exchange (not your keys, not your crypto)

10. Close exchange once Crypto is removed & wallet is double-checked for proof of funds
11. (BONUS) Exchanging to XMR & back into another crypto can clean your trail of the coins

Resources

Websites & resources for you:

- coinmarketcap.com
- coingecko.com
- cryptositeslist.com
- coindesk.com
- cryptotrader.tax
- **getmonero.org (full community, full of resources)**

Exchanges (U.S. Based):

- Binance
- Gemini
- Poloniex
- Kraken
- CEX io
- Crypto.com

Exchanges (Non-U.S.):

- Huobi
- Changelly
- Coinmama
- KuCoin
- Bitfinex
- Uniswap (highly recommend for fast anonymous exchange)
- PoliDex

Exchanges Non-KYC:

- ChangeNow
- LocalMonero
- Kucoin
- Tradeogre
- Crypto ATMs (physical ATMs that accepts crypto)
- Uniswap

Wallets:

- MetaMask (app & browser extension) (Brave/ Chrome web store) (metamask.io)
- Exodus Wallet (app) (exodus.com)
- Cake Wallet (app, personal privacy focused) (cake-wallet.com)
- Ledger Nano (hardware wallet) (ledger.com)
- Monero Official GUI (found on official get-monero.org)
- Lobstr (Stellar Network wallet) (lobstr.co)

Crypto interest bearing storage (crypto banks/ lenders):

- Nexo (nexo.io)
- Crypto.com (crypto.com)
- BlockFi (blockfi.com)

Telegram channels I use:

- Monero XMR : t.me/monero
- Monero Mining: t.me/xmrmine
- Monero Orange Pills: t.me/MoneroOrangePills
- Wownero: t.me/wownero
- Ripple – XRP : t.me/Ripple
- Cryptocurrencies Channel: t.me/cryptocurrency
- **New Age Coin Group : t.me/newagecoingroup**

Tech services to use:

- ProtonMail (email) (protonmail.com)
- StartMail (email) (startmail.com)
- Ctemplar (email) (ctemplar.com)
- Tresorit (encrypted privacy cloud storage) (tresorit.com)
- NordLocker (encrypted privacy cloud storage) (nordlocker.com)
- Nextcloud (self-hosted, open-source cloud storage) (nextcloud.com)
- Mullvad VPN (mullvad.net)
- IVPN (ivpn.net, open-source vpn, accepts crypt payment)
- Proton VPN (protonvpn.com)
- Nord VPN (nordvpn.com)
- Express VPN (only one without a data breach) (expressvpn.com)
- Tor Browser (learn more before using) (torproject.org)
- F-droid (open-source Android app store) (f-droid.org)

- NewPipe (free open-source, add-free YouTube alternative, find in f-droid store) (newpipe.net)
- LBRY (open-source, free speech YouTube alternative) (lbry.com)
- Brave (internet privacy browser) (brave.com)
- Telegram (telegram.org)
- LibreOffice (free open-source alt to Microsoft Office) (libreoffice.org)
- Brax.me & Brax's store through his ".me" website. Find his channel on LBRY to learn more about privacy & spyware free tech. (brax.me)
- The Hated One (privacy focused tech tips and channel, found on LBRY & through New Pipe for YouTube viewing)
- Begin learning about Linux computer operating systems (open-source & privacy replacement to Windows & Apple) (linux.org)
- System76 (system76.com) (Linux based computers & laptops)
- Purism (puri.sm) (Linux based computers, laptops, & phones)
- Start9 Labs (start9.com)
- GloBee (accept crypto payments) (globee.com)
- Mintx (purchase precious metal-backed crypto & trade in for physical metals) (mintx.co)
- Unstoppable Domains (uses .crypto domains built on a blockchain for crypto payments & use of non-censored free-net) (unstoppabledomains.com)

I will be uploading training courses on my website if you wish to follow along and actually see what sources we use & visualize everything. Grab some crypto merch at the site as well & support a fellow crypto fanatic. Every purchase, donation, & tip helps me keep the books & website going. I wouldn't be able to do anything without everyone's support.

Website: newagecoin.net
Telegram: t.me/newagecoingroup

END

Buy me a drink if you really found everything useful.

Monero Tip Address:
89kUHd5EZdt2CVTgxYxWWNinANWgzXeb1PqmUda5Ffx-
QeUT8N8k5WipDqwXtyqebMyZxzD79aCxmAWoK9aT-
nQnXNK3c3DfT